HAIL *to* CALIFORNIA

HAIL *to* CALIFORNIA

The University of California at Berkeley
in Verse and Story

COMPILED BY

Rocky Main '49

CALIFORNIA ALUMNI ASSOCIATION
UNIVERSITY OF CALIFORNIA AT BERKELEY

There are two classes of poets—
the poets by education and practice,
these we respect; and poets
by nature, these we love.

Ralph Waldo Emerson
1874

~

This book is dedicated
to all those individuals
who are "poets by nature"

CONTENTS

VOICES *of* FRIENDS *and* ASSOCIATES

PREFACE

When asked what inspired me to locate poems that had been written about the University of California at Berkeley, I was reminded of Victor Hugo's words: "There is nothing so powerful, not all the armies in the world, as an idea whose time has come."

Chancellor Robert Berdahl, once en route from Sacramento to Oregon, agreed to meet with the Northern C's, the Cal Alumni Club based in Redding, California, my hometown. To enhance my introduction of him, I read my poem "To the Spirit of My Alma Mater" (which appears later in this anthology). After dinner he graciously requested a copy.

Then I started to wonder whether many poems had been written about the University. If such poems existed, where was the repository? I could find none. Thus began my search.

The serendipitous journey through the production of this volume has brought me great joy. Perhaps it was just an idea whose time had come.

Rocky Main

ACKNOWLEDGMENTS

Umberto Eco once wrote that "language is community."
This book is a wonderful sampling of community from
people who have been associated with the University of
California at Berkeley. The selections include the work
of undergraduates, graduates, associates, and friends.

Many people have been involved with breathing life
into this interpretation of *Hail to California*. First I thank
all the poets. Becoming acquainted with members of the
Berkeley family with whom I had no previous contact has
been a true pleasure. One poet responded by e-mail from
Paris! Correspondents have offered words of enthusiasm
and support for this project. I think of them, especially
the graduates, who at one time had written words that
were personally significant and put them in a drawer for
safekeeping. Now those words can be shared. I think of
the busy undergraduates who found time to answer the
call. To each of you I send my affection and appreciation.
Interacting with you has been a joy.

Russell Schoch, editor of the *Cal Monthly*, generously
ran three announcements about the project in the maga-
zine. This contribution was invaluable, as the announcements prompted most of the graduate responses. Nancy
Blattel, also in the CAA office, helped track down essen-

tial information. Mark Appel, Associate Executive Director of the CAA, had the vision and enthusiasm for the project that moved it toward reality. My heartfelt thanks to each of you.

Laura Demir, who teaches creative writing, was my first faculty contact. Her name was given to me by my grandson Matt, who had taken classes from her. She not only encouraged me about the project but also gave me invaluable guidance in contacting other faculty members. She also included information about the project in the Creative Writing Minor News Online. Thanks, Laura. You were wonderful.

Though my ads in the *Daily Cal* were not fruitful, meeting Andy Chau, a student staff member, was a great pleasure. He in turn led me to Marty Gaetjens, Mass Communications, who ran project news in their Online News. Thanks to both of you.

Thank you, Dave Duer and Debbie Tieh, in the Development Office of Doe Library, for providing access to the old *Blue and Gold* yearbooks, making work space available, and facilitating the research process. Harriet Williams, Carole Malkin, and Al Fern helped with selections. If you, dear reader, ever have the inclination, go to the Morrison Library and ask for Alex Warren. Treat yourself to traveling back through time on the Berkeley campus with the *Blue and Golds* as your time machine. You will have a wonderful adventure and learn a lot of history along the way.

Zack Rogow, associated with the School of Education and key person in facilitating the Lunch Poetry Reading series, has been especially helpful in encouraging the undergraduate voice. Thank you, Zack.

Maxine Hong Kingston, whose very name epitomizes that which is good in poetry, kindly participated in the project. Her name adds a special flavor to the collection, for which I am deeply grateful.

Thank you, Class of '49 Torch and Shield members, for your thoughtful input regarding the title selection.

Thanks to David Emmerson and Hampton Hancock, whose wonderful assistance helped bring the original submissions to the cohesiveness of the computer format. It was a pleasure to work with you.

Thank you, Deborah Kirshman, Development Director for the University of California Press and friend of my dear friend Joan Gruen, for guiding me to Christine Taylor of Wilsted and Taylor Publishing Services. Christine and her colleagues Melody Lacina and Melissa Ehn have given their time and talent to make an idea become a beautiful and tangible reality.

Last, but not least, thanks to my family and friends who have listened to me with interest and enthusiasm. I love you.

Perhaps someday a second volume of *Hail to California* will be made possible by the poets we love.

                                                    Rocky Main

Hail to California

Hail to California, Alma Mater dear—
Sing the joyful chorus,
Sound it far and near—
Rallying 'round her banner
We will never fail—
California Alma Mater, Hail! Hail! Hail!

Hail to California, queen in whom we're blest—
Spreading light and goodness
Over all the West,
Fighting 'neath her standard
We shall sure prevail—
California Alma Mater, Hail! Hail! Hail!

Clinton "Brick" Morse
1907

March 23—In my office at school

I am out on my 4th-floor balcony.
If it were not for poetry,
I wouldn't've unjammed the doors,
and be standing amongst the rooftops.
Green hills surround me and the green
copper eaves. A green copper pineapple
caps the Library—Welcome. Welcome.
Down through an immense copper-framed skylight,
I can see a bookroom where I've never been.
The Campanile bongs and echoes into my nook.
I have been here a long time. Since I was young.
And the nearest buildings and the biggest trees,
the oldest trees also here long ago.
In the hills, away from trees, are the recent blocking
        cement structures—probably labs.
Sounds of planes and air conditioning.
Breezes touch me.
Clanging of dropped sewerpipes.
I should feel nostalgia for times gone but
I have this vista. This vista is my own.
        This place mine for staying till old.

Maxine Hong Kingston '62
ENGLISH

VOICES *of the* PAST

✦✦

Excerpts from The Blue and Gold
1877–1924

Dedication

To the Alumni of the U.C.

To you, who trod the selfsame paths of lore
    In which our upward journey we pursue
    And strive to reach the prize so fair to view,—
The heights on which Fame's golden sunbeams pour
Their radiant wealth; to you, who midst the roar
    Of worldly strife, to Alma Mater true,
    Look back, your eyes suffused with loving dew,
And long for college days and hopes once more
To you, whose lives and deeds our hearts inspire,
    With emulation fresh, anew to cope
        With tow'ring obstacles that would abate
Our ardor; yes, with every fond desire,
    O fratres, and with every joyous hope,
        To you our BLUE AND GOLD we dedicate.

The Editors

25

Senior Class of First Term 1877–78

In the student history of our University, we have occupied a peculiar place. We are the connecting link between the times when Berkeley was the home not only of hard working but high-spirited students, who made college life a reality, and the time when a mushroom civilization has destroyed our beautiful landscape, and rapid transit unites our students to the greater but less student-like attractions of the neighboring cities. "*O tempora! O mores!*" Times have changed! The mirthful chorus and the "flow of soul" have almost deserted fair Berkeley; and worse, nothing worthy of student life has taken their places. It would be rather hard to say that scholarship even has improved since those days. Then there were strong bodies and vigorous minds here; men that could take a hand (!) in anything, and do it with a relish, too. When we are gone, those times will be known in Berkeley only by tradition, and ere long their memories will be lost in oblivion.

A younger generation is crowding us off the stage of college life, and even thus will it be hereafter. We quit these scenes with mingled feelings of joy and sadness—joy, to be up and doing for ourselves; sadness, that we must separate ourselves from the associations which, if we do not feel them now to be the happiest of our lives, we are almost certain to do so hereafter.

A. F. Morrison
Class Historian
1878

Cram, cram, cram,
From the rosy dawn till night,
    Cram, cram, cram,
From the dewy eve till light.

    Cram, cram, cram,
In the sunshine's ruddy glare,
    Cram, cram, cram,
By the candle's fitful flare.

    Cram, cram, cram,
On the coffee's bracing draught,
    Cram, cram, cram,
When the strength'ning brandy's quaffed.

    Cram, cram, cram,
With a towel 'round thy brow,
    Cram, cram, cram,
While thy feet in mustard bow.

    And thus it is I cram
'Till I wish I'd ne'er been born,
    For that beastly mathematics Ex.
That comes to-morrow morn.

                    1884

And now, '86, I bid you farewell;
On thy merits I no longer shall dwell.
No bard thou dost need thy praises to sing;
But always, as now, may the college ring
With the praise of this Class, 'till Seniors, at last,
They cast their eyes backward, back to the past,
And the youngest class to their mind recalls,
How, as Freshmen, they came to Berkeley's halls.

G. F. Bigelow
Class Historian
1884

Cornelius

October's days were waning fast,
As into Berkeley's vale there passed
A crank, who bore, in puny fame,
The ever-since detested name,
   Cornelius.

His brow was beaming with a grin—
Exterior fair of what within
Proved disappointing, flat and tame.
As English Tutor came this same
   Cornelius.

His classes in due time he met;
And hopeful, too, were they as yet
Of much substantial gain. Hope vain!
Observe how acted in the main
   Cornelius.

"You cannot pass," to some he said:
"A word misspelled in short has led
You into ruin: such mistake
Is grievous, vital, vile." Thus spake
   Cornelius.

"Here is a theme bound with a string;
The Faculty forbids this thing—
Fault is it of such gravity."
So said, with smirking suavity,
   Cornelius.

Continued he, "this comma frail
Has not sufficient length of tail;

For this I yet must 'cinch' one more."
Procedure foolish even for
        Cornelius.

"Above this 'i' there is no dot;
To cross your 't' you here forgot;
Another still must fail,"—and smiled,
While uttering dictum since reviled,
        Cornelius.

"In themes is careful thought of worth?"
A student asked. Reply came forth:
"Good thought but little here avails,
"If you neglect these small details."
        Cornelius!!

Two years 'mid such ideas we spend;
And then kind Fates slight solace send.
With feelings glad and gay we thank
The one that frees us from this crank,
        Cornelius.
              1885

Both Sides

I do not see why [affiliated] colleges of Divinity and Theology
may not be established at Berkeley, or at any other place
that their founders may think wise.
PRESIDENT'S BIENNIAL REPORT, 1886

The preacher and the deacon have been up in arms
    and squeakin',
  And a-cursing at the Berkeley boys like mad;
'Tis said they're not religious, that their drinking is
    prodigious,
  And their general conduct altogether bad.

Now Deacon Zachariah (living just outside Ukiah),
  Says the 'Varsity will ne'er get boy of his,
"For by the great John Cotton the whole darned place
    is rotten,
  And the De'il himself has made it what it is."

So the dear lad gets his knowledge in some theologic
    college,
  Where they bring 'em up to love and fear the Lord;
But behind their church and praying I feel confident in
    saying,
  That their pranks were of a kind to be abhorred;

That for sneaking and for meanness and the whole
    scale of uncleanness,
  They were just as bad as ever they do make 'em,
And their pious wily tricking should have brought
    them many a licking—
  Why, up here we most summarily would shake 'em.

Now you crusty old tormentors, be you High Church
    or Dissenters,

We read bibles for the wisdom they will bring;
We frown on fights and quarrels and believe in
    Christian morals,
  But Geology is quite a different thing.

We shall spurn your ancient bias, however you decry us,
  Though we hope some day to reach the Pearly Gate;
We can stand a little lying when it's high poetic flying,
  As for Science—we prefer to take it straight.

The truth we shouldn't smother; we weren't built for
    one another,
  (And I think you're cute enough to stay away);
'Twixt us two in creation there's no more "affiliation"
  Than there is between an eagle and a jay.

Can there be "affiliation" or be reconciliation?
  Now what's the use in trying to be nice?
They don't like our way of teaching; we hate
    antediluvian preaching;
  And the crafty scheme it isn't worth its price.

If this blessed institution is to teach us evolution,
  Why, let 'em know it and leave 'em to their ease.
Then here's to Berkeley College for it's there we get our
    knowledge,
  And the parsons they can go just where they please.

1888

To the University of California

Sweet Mother, Berkeley by the Sea,
At thy proud name we bend the knee;
We hail thee queen, the hills thy throne,
Thy crown the love thy children own.

Like some clear beacon through the night
Thy splendor floods with radiant light
This golden land. From East and West
Thy children rise and call thee blest.

Long live! long teach each loyal heart
To love and live the better part.
Long hold thy regnant place and be
Our Mother, Berkeley by the Sea.

Bertha T. Bradley
1894

Pom-tiddy-om-pom-pay!!!

Some Stanford guys came up to-day—
   Pom-tiddy-om-pom! Pom-tiddy-om-pom!
Thought they'd show us how to play—
   Pom-tiddy-om-pom-pay!!
But when Pete, or Smith, or Hall
   Pom-tiddy-om-pom! Pom-tiddy-om-pom!
Bucked the line or rushed the ball,
   Pom-tiddy-om-pom-pay!!
Stanford's little Willie-boys
   Pom-tiddy-om-pom! Pom-tiddy-om-pom!
Shut their heads and stopped their noise!
   Pom-tiddy-om-pom-pay!!

   Chorus:
   Oh, what fun we've had since it was done!
   Murphy *kicked* the air!
   Fisher tore his hair!
   When they heard us counting up the score!
   Pom-tiddy-om-pom! Pom-tiddy-om-pom!
     Pom-tiddy-om-pom-pay!!

I met a girl all dressed in red—
   Pom-tiddy-om-pom! Pom-tiddy-om-pom!
"Stanford'll win!" That's what she said.
   Pom-tiddy-om-pom-pay!!
I met that same girl after the game.
   Pom-tiddy-om-pom! Pom-tiddy-om-pom!
She didn't seem to think the same.
   Pom-tiddy-om-pom-pay!!
I said, "Stanford's full of tacks."
   Pom-tiddy-om-pom! Pom-tiddy-om-pom!
"Oh," she said, "you *Garry'd* the axe!!"
   Pom-tiddy-om-pom-pay!!

Chorus:

Oh, what fun! That's how those guys were done.
You see, they brought their axe!
But we made all the whacks!
All we had to do was simply this:
Pom-tiddy-om-pom! Pom-tiddy-om-pom!
    Pom-tiddy-om-pom-pay!!

I went out to the game to-day—
    Pom-tiddy-om-pom! Pom-tiddy-om-pom!
Watched our boys begin to play—
    Pom-tiddy-om-pom-pay!!
A Stanford man said, "I'll bet ten!"
    Pom-tiddy-om-pom! Pom-tiddy-om-pom!
Of course I took his bet up then.
    Pom-tiddy-om-pom-pay!!
Then our boys began to smash—
    Pom-tiddy-om-pom! Pom-tiddy-om-pom!
Well,—I didn't lose my cash!
    Pom-tiddy-om-pom-pay!!

Chorus:

Oh, what fun! Around the end they run!
The Stanford crowd looked sad!
The Berkeley crowd looked glad!
When our boys went banging into them,—'twas
Pom-tiddy-om-pom! Pom-tiddy-om-pom!
    Pom-tiddy-om-pom-pay!!

1900

The North Hall Steps

The North Hall steps are crowded tight;
   The "mob" is always there.
Adown the path the co-eds flock;
   And the "mob" is always there.

No Profs attempt to mount these steps,
   Whene'er the "mob" is there,
For stern tobacco fumes forbid,
   Whene'er the "mob" is there.

The North Hall stairs are full of boys;
   The "mob" is always there.
And North Hall boys are full of stares,—
   O that "mob," it's always there.

Some girls think it's just too sweet,
   Because the "mob" is there.
But others think it's awful mean,
   Because the "mob" is there.

But would our College be complete,
   If the "mob" were never there?
Nay! In future years our hearts will turn
   To this "mob" that hangs out there.

1900

Greeting

Just a magic-lantern show,
  Friends, is all we offer you.
The swiftly-rushing college year is fled,
And fled its Junior joys; but, as it sped,
Some scenes we caught, the truest, dearest, which behold
Shining upon the pages of the Blue and Gold!
One fleeting picture now is on the screen,
But turn the page, and lo! you change the scene.
The stately pageant of solemnity,
The antic pranks of college jollity,
The noisy mad delight of victory,
And sorrow of defeat,
The callow Freshman new from country school,
Instructor, co-ed, hero, dig, and fool,
Successively you greet;
Till the last page is turned, till the last slide
Has flashed its picture, and is laid aside:
The show is done;
And soon, as other interests appear,
And year of life is added unto year,
The very thought and memory of it is gone.

It may be that, some day, some man whom age
Has bowed, or woman snowy-haired, shall turn the page
Where this is writ;
A start, a thrill of pleasure at the view!
The Blue and Gold of Nineteen Hundred Two!
And thus the aged one shall sit,
And live the well-loved scenes again;
Ah! we were class-mates then!
The magic lantern! magic then in truth,

Which on the screen of age throws the dear scenes of youth!
Gently then will criticize
They who read with moistened eyes!
Gently criticize, we pray,
You who read our work to-day!
Only pictures fixed ere flying,
Only blossoms plucked ere dying,
Mingled rosemary and rue,
Friends, 'tis these we offer you!
The Blue and Gold of Nineteen Hundred Two.

1902

The Cushion Tea

The Co-eds gave a Cushion Tea,
    To help their sports along;
And what they did, and how 'twas done,
    Is the burden of my song.

The pillows were solicited
    From Co-ed clubs galore;
And candy in abundance, too,
    To gain your cash the more.

The Kappa Alpha Thetas sent
    A cushion, all so nice,
Embroidered in the finest style
    With cunning little mice.

The Prytaneans' pillow was
    Adorned with college views,
'Twas pretty near the only thing
    They've made you'd care to use.

The choral pillow, very loud,
    Had many bars to rest;
Although it sold so low, they say,
    It brought of notes the best.

The cushion of the H. D. I.
    Was backstitched all around,
With buttonholes and unmatched stripes
    And darns that have no sound.

The archery club's donation has
    Just set all hearts a-quiver;

The eds are striving valiantly,
    Their victims to deliver.

The maids who study chemistry
    Sent a pillow, I confess,
Adorned with flasks and test tubes, and
    Perfumed with H_2S.

The girls all dressed in old-time style,
    Their hair all powdered white,
And danced the stately minuet,
    Until the shades of night.

But, of all the evening's features, the
    Most touching one, no doubt,
Was their guileless way of charging
    You ten cents to get out.

1902

Pierce in Debate

There's a quick electric motion,
And a rapid locomotion,
And we all attain the notion,
 Pierce has risen for debate.

With a pair of fiery glances,
As one foot now quick advances,
While the air his finger lances,
 Pierce is ready for debate.

At three hundred words a minute,
As if speed were bound to win it—
"Dicey, Bodley, Taine," begin it,—
 Pierce has opened his debate.

  Words come out like scintillations—
  "'Lection, min'stry, cit'zens,
   nations"—
  Ever faster variations:
   Pierce proceeds in his debate.

  Meteor-like the show of phrases!
  Lightning flash of hands in mazes!
  How the peroration dazes!
   Pierce has ended his debate.

       1902

Lament

Restless shades of Billy Friend!
    They have painted old North Hall;
This sacrilege will never end,—
    Soon the campus they will spoil.

We'd forgotten Stanford's boldness
    When she stole the Senior C;
We had even borne her coldness
    When we won the great trophy.

But the very hardest trial
    We must bear, when truth is said,
Is—there's no use in denial,
    They have painted North Hall *red*!

1902

Bill and Others

Sing a song of pleasure
    A wagon full of beer,
With three and thirty frat men
    Getting full of cheer.

Whisper a song of naughtiness—
    A tin pail full of paint,
The shingles of the Kappa house
    Assumed a reddish taint.

Chant a song of labor—
    A benzine keg or two
And Theta Delt and Delta Tau
    At dawn—and sulphur blue.

Howl a song of giddy roast,
    Of omelette, broil and fry—
Bill Finley's dread official pen
    An' bawl-out in his eye.

Moan a song of repentance deep,
    Of three and thirty heads,
Of two hitherto unprofaned frats
    And a color scheme in reds.

1904

Even the Profs Worked

The faculty men, on Labor Day,
Were strong for getting the weeds away

From the lawn in front of their Faculty Club.
But how did they get there?   That's the rub.

Here you see pictured a bunch of four
Ready to work till their limbs grow sore;

Only too anxious to get to work,
They hasten along, nor stop to shirk;

On many a pony of many a breed,
Anxious to pull the noxious weed,

Wildly they race for the Club-house door,
And then—Maud Muller don't count no more.

For our faculty men, for grace and brawn,
Have got Maud skinned at mowing a lawn.

1905

A Plea for Sanctity

Being a speech made by Cliff Canfield at his
inauguration as Y.M.C.A. vice-president

Why should we have a "Football Show"?
    The aged Senior asks.
Why should we have professors
    For to oversee our tasks?
Why should we have a football team,
    When but fifteen can play?
When girls can cook, and men can work
    And sweat on Labor Day?
Why should we have our rallies
    When the townsfolk come and smile?
Why can't we go to chapel
    Every night and pray awhile?

1915

The Vanished Lottery

When we went wooing, ages since, we learned the
    lady's views
      Concerning churches, dances, books, or expurgated
      news;
We thrilled to hear her talk about the topics of the day,
      Like Dickens' newest novelette, or Browning's
      sweetest play.
'Twas joy enough for us to see the damsel of our choice.
      It didn't matter WHAT she said, we liked to hear her
      voice.
We took her inner views on faith, we wooed and won
    and wed,
      Before we had the vaguest glimpse of what was in her
      head.

It's different now—these modern girls discuss with pith
    and zest
      The things their grandmas didn't know—or kept
      inside the chest.
The fresh young voices prate of sin, the social evil vice,
      And divers other vital things which aren't considered
      "nice."
The swain who woos in days like these, no doubt can
    plague or vex—
      He knows his darling's inmost thoughts on every
      phase of sex.

Our ancient charmers—bless their hearts—did so
    devise their dress
      That of the things they wore beneath no manly man
      might guess.

They showed us hooped and flouncy frocks, which
    perfect forms revealed.
  The men were fooled, deceived, beguiled, by
    imperfections thus concealed.
We had to marry ere we knew what ladies really wore—
  At least no righteous male dared own he'd found it out
    before.

But nowadays, the modest maid rejoices to display,
  Her raiments' inner mysteries adown the broad
    highway.
Serene, unblushing, calm and cool, to passers-by she
    shows
  The ribbons of her brassiere, the texture of her hose.
Chemise and slip and knickers, too, the modern fashion
    bares—
  None save a blind man now need wed, unknowing
    what she wears.

We paid our court to maids whose forms escaped our
    avid gaze,
  Who cheated nature's lines and curves in many
    cunning ways.
If they wore freckles on their arms—as damsels often did—
  These sweet defects, like dearer charms, remained
    securely hid.
They showed their faces, bared their hands, revealed a
    furtive shoe,
  But bow-legged, knock-kneed, stout or slim,—we wed
    'em ere we knew.

But days of yore no longer are; the present womankind
  Displays most everything she has, each single curve
    and line.

No modern lover raves about his ladies' lips or eyes.
  Why should he? He's a connoisseur of ankles, knees
    and thighs.
The mysteries we wed to solve are cleared at tea or dance.
  THANK GOD! A MAN CAN MARRY NOW
  AND NEVER TAKE A CHANCE.

1918

Song of the Campus Politician

I'm a campus politician
    With an ax to grind;
With a manner unpatrician
    And a one-track mind.
Oh, I never foster malice
    Through effete commands;
On my palm has grown a callous
    Just from shaking hands.

I can grow enthusiastic
    When the need impels,
But my mind is very plastic
    And my thinking cells
Will conform to contradictions
    With an ease sublime—
Oh, I never have convictions
    Till past voting time!

Sincerity's discarded
    And one just pretends;
Why, if progress is retarded
    I discard old friends.
These faults will not have mattered
    Unrecalled, these sins,
When my vest is well-bespattered
    With the honor pins!

You will have my approbation,
    I will share your woes
If you give me indication

How your ballot goes.
I'm the friend of everybody,
    I'm the glad-hand king.
Oh, my morals may be shoddy—
    But the vote's the thing!

D.G.
1922

A Broader View

When sines and cosines lull the brain
To coma, and you strive in vain
To masticate the foreign sounds
Your language master stern expounds,
When lofty learning's stately halls
Seem prisons for ambition's thralls,
Desert them and, in things mundane,
Find truer inspiration then.

'Tis sweet relief to note the flight
Of co-eds togged in colors bright,
To feel the cooling ocean breeze,
To hear its whisper in the trees.
The grandeur of the verdant hills
One's soul with high ideals fills,
And nature's very vastness then
Will draw you to your fellow men.

Seek out your fellows. Grasp the hand
Of men and women both. Expand!
Forget sophistic wiles of sex,
Which only muddle and perplex.
Forget the barriers of wealth
And poverty. Let mutual wealth
Be that of kindness, service too.
Be bigger! Find a broader view!

Drink heartily at nature's rill,
At friendship's fountain drink your fill,
And let fraternal feeling steep

The ego from your mental heap.
Resume your studies. Class and hall
Will then no longer bore nor pall.
Desire for service will replace
False ambition's artifice.

1924

Swan Song!

We're of the show, we know it all,
We've gathered erudition;
We now take our last curtain call
And give our last rendition
Of all the songs we hum so well.
We feel moist about the eyes,
Under our breath we mutter "Hell"
In vain try to disguise
That we've a lump up in our throats
And a sorrowful aching heart,
When we realize we've spoke our piece
And played our final part,
With a dumbish line or a witty one—
A smile—a laugh—a grin!
Clear the stage! Bring new puppets on!
Let another play begin!

1924

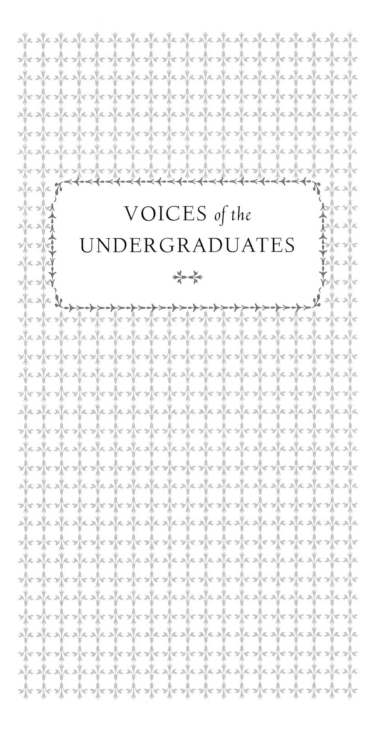

VOICES *of the*
UNDERGRADUATES

❧

Note to Self

And they'll tell you your future is bright,
You, about to embark on the rest of your life.
Focus on careers
Changing worlds like
Changing dirty diapers of
Children shaped like 401 K's and Saturday night at
   home.
They'll tell you that this moment is for reflecting on the
   work to be done.
Write down your goals and paste them to your palms
So that everything you touch feels like promise.
This is what they told me . . .

But I've got a rib cage full of rainy Decembers.
And Tuesdays filled with poetry tucked behind my ears.
I've been writing down the Fridays with the Saturdays
   and stuffing them in my socks for years.
They warm the puddle-dunked shoes that bear my books
   off to class, conveniently folding into paper cranes
   to dry themselves in the wind.
On my right arm I taped the definition of the word
   "ecumenical."
But on my left I have instructions on how to make my
   voice lose its shake when I ask questions in class.
Below the elbow I will write down how to get my
   cheeks not to blush when I figure that out.
I swallowed a picture of a broken heart.
I slept past lunches and stitched all those daydreams into
   a blanket for my shoulders.
I never learned how to drive a stick shift, but I have a
   note that says I tried, crammed in the broken
   taillight of a Honda Civic.

I've got a backpack full of instructions on how to
     cultivate fertile 19-year-old self-slaughter and
     reconstruction.
On the backs of my eyelids I wrote down midnight
     promises of commitment to Organic Chemistry
     that I broke at 5pm promptly.
But yesterday I saw a man dressed in rain, begging for
     change on my way to econ class.
And I don't think I have a place to put that.

I didn't come here to fill my hands with tomorrows,
Rather to collect and shape the character of my
     yesterdays.

Somewhere it happens
That switch from what you will be, to what you are.

So in that becoming,
Collect your yesterdays and unfold them, for all of
     tomorrow to see.

Lay them out before you as you walk, so that they always
     cover the ground beneath your feet.
Then take all the tomorrows and papier-mâché the moon.
Do it with superglue so that your hands get stuck in the sky.
Next curl your toes tight around the scraps of yesterdays
And swell like the tides,
Pulled forever between all that you've been and all you'll
     become.
Now,
Never be anything but today.

Emily Kagan '04
ANTHROPOLOGY/PUBLIC HEALTH/
BIO-BEHAVIORAL PSYCHOLOGY

I didn't see the tanks

I didn't see the tanks
Or the guns and the flowers.
Mario lives in newsprint
In grainy photos, historic power.

Immortalized media moments
Persisting to this day
—"So you're off to Berkeley?"
—"Watch out," people say.

But have those years ended,
Memories faded away?
Does the Cal of yesteryear
Still resemble Cal today?

Bright young minds still pass
Through green Sather Gate
Some sauntering, some rushing,
Some still perennially late.

Students from around the world
Still come to walk these halls
One can cross Cal end to end
And hear English not at all.

Now filled with dino bones
But still looking o'er the bay
The Campanile marks the time
Bells pealing through foggy days.

Telegraph still sprawls
That strange street out of time

Hobos, hippies, and hemp?
Not much changed since—oh, 1969.

The protests now are different
Or maybe they're the same
Different country, different people
But still the same old game.

For all the years that come and go
For all things that persist
Grant Cal the wisdom to change what should
And all else—to resist!

Karen M. Williams '04

ENGLISH

From the Notes of One Berkeley Humanities Student at the Turn of the Century

We are in it together,
    joined by walls, words, bodies set to mark time
    imposed on centuries, days, hysteria, asphalt,
        risk and martyrdom
    pencaps, and crumpled plane tickets. For this
        we are changed.

We speak ten languages
    in a seven bedroom house on so many Streets and
        Avenues
    we are in love with the idea, and its heartbreak.

There is sweat on our brow as we watch
    the screening of a revolutionary film for the first time,
    front lines and backlash, the Patriot Act versus the
        Patriotic Activist,
FSM on a deadline, discernment and the cultivation of
        public disillusionment.

We aspire to tweed and imported espresso on Wheeler's
        sixth floor,
    symbols of the simultaneous intimidation and
        inspiration
    of those professionally crowded minds,
    and their ability to supersede glamour with the lowly
        price
    of conversation and a paper crown.

We look for each other on the bookshelves,
    and in constitutional fortunes, over bridges, and plastic
        oak desks swallowed

into scribbled rows along the lining of Moffit's
underbelly.
In young and blind audacity, vindication, conviction
rubbed raw,
human shrapnel on Telegraph, our walking histories,
our live theses,

And in one Greek semicircle of stone,
filled with our passing mortality, caught
in the shade of so many redwoods
in the shadow of the campanile
against the late October sun.
We testify to the passage of time, we have
become all at once and none at all:
anarchist, capitalist, communist,
separatist, socialist, atheist, environmentalist, feminist.
Artist.

Jes Zychowicz '04
ENGLISH LITERATURE

How

I saw the best minds of my generation ripen in madness,
     starving, hysterical to cultivate naked truths,
dragging science poem idea song through their minds
     day night dawn looking for an angry fix,
angelheaded heads and hearts burning for an ancient
     heavenly creation in the starry dynamo in the
     machinery of thought,
who sat up smoking, looking to Saint Francis—but never
     Saint Jude—and contemplating farmhouses and
     constellations,
who didn't understand unhappiness and sobbed in
     Union Square over unfeeling and the revival of
     feelings,
who cast themselves in documentaries every night on
     Ridge Road for twenty minutes, stopping
     production only for the 11 o'clock dating shows,
who messily scrawled poems in two parts, with two
     speakers spitting two points, to perform at
     performance parties,
who lay, resting head on bended arm, listing possible
     names for possible children,
who defined was as what was wrote groundbreaking
     teen romances that were just tiny reflections of
     what they felt was and may be,
who cast themselves as characters in perfect pop songs,
     as seasoned song stage veterans, while humming
     mindless tunes,
who performed one-act plays on the way to Longs on
     Broadway to buy sweatpants,
who wrote twangy love songs on untuned guitars to girls
     with pretty eyes and smoked Marlboro Lights

because that's as country-western as you can be in
the city,
who calculated alpha sigma theta but couldn't calculate
simple equations adding one plus the other,
who ran through museums destroying art, or at least
considered it for a brief moment,
who were sad to speak without a hint of aggression,
who regretted ever wanting to regret and stayed up on
strict sleep schedules to study up on how to cure
the world of its insignificance,
who dreamed up correspondences with mysterious
benefactors on flea market typewriters, detailing
intellectual adeptness and progress in coming-
of-age,
who wanted affirmation and acknowledgment and
reassurance about pursuits they felt completely
affirmed and acknowledged and reassured about,
who were interviewed in twenty years and recorded in
words that put horrible amounts of importance on
the times and people involved,
words that rose skillfully to embody a movement of
geniuses, child prodigies, and gods,
with the absolute heart of the poem evolving still as a
perpetual work in progress . . .

Kat Malinowska '05
MASS COMMUNICATIONS/ENGLISH

Perspective

My poetry professor instructed
us to write from the point of view
of the opposite sex, asked
that I write as a woman: maybe
about Monistat 7, I brainstormed,
split ends, childbirth, or breaking
my fictional hymen, but I couldn't
help but return to the time when at
twelve I wore my mother's pearls
and felt their weight as pleasant
as a stream against my collarbone,
or the way I would lie stomach-down
on my kitchen floor singing to Aretha,
my feet circling through the air like
unattended children, or about that time
I shrieked when Angela first kissed
Jordan Catalano and I fanned my face
in disbelief, or even how every Monday
and Wednesday last year I would sit outside
Kroeber Hall for hours thinking he must
notice me now as I attempted to appear
deep in thought the way people often do
with furrowed eyebrows and crossed legs;
I couldn't help but think of the way I will
stare out my bedroom window on nights
he is away, and concern will drape over
my face the way it will for mothers who
look out their own bedroom windows and
feel as if they have given birth to this world,
and that it has taken too long for it to return home.

* * *

So you see,
writing from a woman's point
of view, Mr. Reed,
like asking the blind
to describe darkness or the poor hunger,
would be asking of me
to write honestly.

Angelo Nikolopoulos '05
PSYCHOLOGY/ENGLISH/EDUCATION

Pantoum

While we are young in Berkeley,
let us enjoy more than one another,
but the city, that generous way it has,
opened up like a long strand of light.

Let us enjoy more than just the company, the splendor,
    of one another,
more than our arms entwined, an infinite chance for love,
entangled like a long strand of light,
more than anything between us.

More than our arms entwined as we walk on Telegraph,
    some prophecy for love—
what the city is, I'll admit, we could never be.
It is more than anything between us, of us, us.
You should wonder, too: what can we give back?

What the city is, you must admit, we could never be.
It enfolds us like the deep arms of a spirit, a loved one
    returned,
so what can we, two slight lovers, give?
Being young, it is true we'd rather admire it, sitting in
    the rain, quietly.

The deep arms of a spirit wrap around us, loved ones
    returning
to the city and that generous way it has,
and because we are somewhat in love we would rather
    admire it, in the morning mist, and quietly,
while we are young and entwined, in splendor, in
    Berkeley.

Olivia Friedman '06
ENGLISH/CREATIVE WRITING

Testament to the visionistically twisted

In the 21 years of my existence
I have shifted through this city
know that Berkeley—
finest dream America has ever had
I awaken to find that
walking around with the memory of an idea
is not enough to manifest a reality
we want to march on Telegraph
with backwards lack of us just because
we try to touch glory days
taste tear gas and say
something that might somehow
save the cause
the very warfare
we fight with guerilla poetry
unaware there are stool pigeons
who lurk inside our classrooms
hell/even our bedrooms

I had a co-op housemate who said
all single parent family homes create
alcoholic drones/drug addicts/criminal foes
who should never be unleashed
as they can flourish nowhere but in poverty

(not knowing she was addressing me)

I take each opportunity to stab this paper
as if this pen might somehow
indent her flesh
every last syllable is relative
within this space

it is difficult to differentiate
between those who are down
and those who are up
idle individuals don't get it

you're a part of a solution
or you equal the problem
those who bust out to solve them
for we fill each piece with forums
to speak it like we see it
bold and impressionistic
precise/I derive
from blood of write
to lip this life into its next slight drive
nothing is more contrived than
certain people I've encountered
a co-worker once said
real women plan their pregnancies
and they have to breast feed
in order to be productive members of society,
and well, single mothers,
they just shouldn't be.
when I hear these things, I'm like
this is Berkeley, right?

we rep with UC sweat shop shirts concealed
in some mad dash to keep it surreal
I'm starting to feel like this is the place
where all the village idiots flee
bent on infecting me with illogicality
although it is their very disease
that injects me
con este vista mia
para decir la poesía
en contra de cada pendejo

que quiere venderse a la ley de escribir
porque yo digo
la manifestación de yo misma
in any tongue I twist it
just to kick it to those who cannot view the visionistic

last Sunday I saw a poster plastered on a pole
      if they go to war
      we riot
somebody has to translate for me
an ability to promote peace via street violence

Galeano says misfortune is not a question of fate
we're back in the hard place and
only rock it since we believe we belong here

even on this campus where pro-life punks meander
in front of Sather Gate
with images of aborted fetuses
What is the point in free speech
if we are not at liberty to act on
things they free-speak about?
social retards wave pamphlets in my face
I wonder if the only mistake woman ever made was
their mothers not having abortions when they were
     pregnant with them
demonstrators spit contradictions from misguided mouths
partial-aborted brains deny the obvious
When 77% of anti-abortion leaders are men
100% of them will never be pregnant.
double standard bastards exercise rights to free will
still can't grasp the vagina laissez-faire

black kettles circulate a palm that only
knows one kind of change

we search/attempt to tap into vision of 3rd eye
while this revelation gives me like 4 & 5
so many eyes
others cannot perceive
got to count to infinity

idiotic commentaries are lyrical ammunition
for poets who inscribe rites to free will
what will be will be evident
since nothing
and no one
can prevent
the verbal movement
from spitting

Cassandra Tesch '06
SPANISH/PORTUGUESE

The Legend of Tolman Hall

Rumor has it the architect committed suicide
because of this complaint refrain—
Why are educators relegated
to the ugliest university edifices?
But history tells a different tale
of imitation Swiss
design and architectural accolades.

We'll settle for the easy answer:
to prepare for long-lived careers
in "portable buildings" three times
our age, unfit for prisoners.

Already, we've learned to expect
no compensation
for seismic unsoundness and aesthetic antithesis
on the inside of Tolman.
We plan extra time to be on time
to a room that may not exist.

Among the luminaries here now
or here then,
it is not poet Robert Hass, nor
essayist Joan Didion, nor even childhood
favorite Beverly Cleary that I want to meet.
Please, pull me from my literary inclinations
to architecture, and make me a date with the late
Gardner A. Dailey

So I can ask:

Where have you hidden the missing numbers?
Or are there rooms accessible only through magical

wardrobes and train station walls?
Don't you see we are living testament
to your building's namesake—leader in the psychological
experiment involving rat and maze,
constantly beating our heads on dead ends
preparing to teach in a maze
to amaze.

Jill E. Thomas '06
GRADUATE STUDENT/EDUCATION

This University

Pack my past into bags and carry an empty stomach
into this University
I spin in circles, stare at buildings, can't breathe in the
enormity of this University

days pass in my tiny room packed in by closets and ten
feet walls stuck
but a roommate smiles and I am no longer lost in the
abyss of the University

and familiar trees outstretch their weeping willow
limbs to me and hang childhood memories
maybe I can be seven again and just sit under the trees
and dream in a kid's University

after sips and chugs four fresh-faced females stumble
through a clutter of street names
new girlfriends walk crooked lines in the dark together
so they don't skip the avenue University

and I met a boy hiding behind open doors in hallways
meant for busy academic brains
but he's all I see, lets my mind my tongue roam free when
we kiss in this University

roommates dine on midnight snacks of laughter while
words flow until sunrise
my eyes open wide while still heavy from sleepless
nights, adrift in the University

* * *

we take notes on how to let tears fall, let laughter roll
off tongues before moments fade,
set aside books and reminders. June floats higher than
education in an imperfect University

June Daniella Lucarotti '07
UNDECLARED

this is a poem called i

I
live at
Le Chateau: a Co-op a block between
People's Park and Willard Park, one or
two up from Telegraph.
Students with fists against the Hand of
Intervention. Intense debates lasting
past Midnight leave you spent as
emotions run as high as the lawsuit the
neighbors have against us.
And I wonder . . .

What is home?

Something I'm trying desperately to
find. Is it the place I began, my mother's
womb, whatever current 6 walls of
confinement put me on my back, to face
its infinite ceiling?
In an insomniatic daze I once called my
sister at 4 am, crying that I don't have a
home, but she said, "*Home is wherever
me and Mom are,*" and although I see
what she means I have to disagree.

For me Home will always be the one life
within us and abroad. We are all
scattered cousins of not so separate
strands. Clans, Tribes, country and city,
cover me in the mystery, because my
home is the planet.

* * *

And if Ethnicity is the "notion of a homeland" that means I'm just one notion after the other. Fractioned like a pie chart of white, brown, and black slices.
Most of me stolen from Africa, doomed to a cotton patch history, Creole depths of the Atlantic.
Some of me, Cheyenne and Cree on this continent since before Columbus, hunting and gathering in the North-eastern forests of Canada.
Rainy England, windmills in the Netherlands, some of me on the merry old Island of Ireland with a thousand shades of green, and even in ice and snow, because my blood is Scandinavian.

I'd like to think that I am the living breathing dream they all had, a dream to be free.
I never thought this would be confirmed at the Chat by a dirty street girl up from Telegraph, her speech broken by the bottle of Mickey's beer on her breath as she
says,
"*I'm sorry if you're born here. You should get to sleep at any church or any field anywhere.*" Someone asks,
"*Why do you have to be born here, is it about being American?*"
"*I meant if you're born on this planet . . . You don't own the land, the land*

owns you." She says this sincerely,
responding quickly, and it makes my
hair tingle with the ceaselessly stirring
blood of my ancestors. The air thick with
suspense asked of us one moment of
silence.
None of us could deny that what she said
was true. The earth will cover us long
after we've covered it, just like the
House I live in. Layers of fresh white
paint that cover years of talking walls,
art yelling out, not just graffiti of the
incoherent.

We are ears and eyes listening looking
out to the world, willing to talk until all
is said, and a slight hum of
understanding always lingers when each
good conversation ends. My housemates
are Happy Tears, if I could give them a
big hug all at once, I would do it every
day. Eyes bright and character to match,
it's more than just a pursuit of beautiful
bodies, but home. Home in their
eyebrows, lips, hips, and smiles. Home
in the lessons they teach me of love.
Home in Buddy the cat, when he's in the
garden. Our kitchen, meals, food
deliveries, even home in the endless
cigarette butts, Old Crow Whiskey, dirty
plates spoons and mugs.
One of my housemates cried and said
that this is the only place she's been able
to call home in a long time. I hadn't

expected it, but I cried too. She was
born in Estonia, daughter of an
important man in the Soviet Army. I
remember she once told us how as a
small girl she used to tell him, "War is
stupid," and I want to know what it
sounded like in her language. Her voice
sweet and resilient.
We sit by our pool, and I wish I could
tell her something helpful, but instead I
listen. I know that she is still that little
girl and so am I.
Sitting up straight in courtrooms that are
smoke-stained living rooms. Wanting to
yell but at times having to suppress even
a whisper.
I know that I can't cry enough tears for
the people that I'll think of in every song
I sing of joy.
"Once upon a time it was a Co-op"
they'll say
But I'll say
*You can take the people out of Le
Chateau
but you can't take Le Chateau out of the
people.*
I'll say it again so you really hear me . . .
You can take the people out of Le Chateau,
but you cannot take Le Chateau out
of the people.

Oh and I want to take this poem to
Ishmael, ride up Hillegass, past People's
Park

smile at that man that plants flowers
each morning, smile at anyone who
lets me and my bike go first, smile at
the Law Enforcement as I veer right off
Bancroft toward his office in the 4th floor of
Wheeler, go in there, and do my best not
to cry like I did at my Aunt Sissy's
church, that one time after 7 years and
she held me and smiled.

And I'll tell him that I don't know what
I'm going to do when he's not there in
his office on Fridays, because
sometimes I feel like no one is listening,
and I know that he always listens. And I
want to tell him how much I hope that,
today, May 6, 2004, is like October 7,
1955, for Allen Ginsberg, when he
sparked the beat generation.
And I want to tell him that *"this is a*
poem called i" is a Tin Can phone with
strings to the heartbeat of the world
Because beyond the notions of
homeland, family, friends, and landscape
Home for me is my voice
And the voices of the timeless few that
listen.

Crazy little world we live in,
every day I hold it, revere it, and taste it,
sweetly
on the tip of my pen

Sharita Towne '07
INTERDISCIPLINARY STUDIES/ART

Tread

The sun cast its reticent light
On the Campanile tower
But the light is a glimpse in time,
An impressionistic masterpiece, painted with watercolors
Fleeting and evanescent

To me it is the portrait of hope
But hope is fleeting
Can disappear with every academic meeting
Every whatchamacall forsaken drama meeting
And yet it comes to symbolize the unlived dream
Impossible as it may seem

This is then my life story
I came here seeking glory
I found myself in the middle of unforeseen circumstance
And took a haughty stance
Many a time I experienced the like

But I was goaded by a drive
A futile drive, quixotic drive to come alive
Ever since last year I witnessed someone my age lose
        her life
Came to talk, came to schmooze
Came to make quick friendship, cannot lose
Crazy days
Blur
Green clover shines through the window when I open
        my eyes
How much have I slept?
Later than ever before
So much to explore, so much to retell,

So much sufficient criteria to coming out of one's shell
So much routine set-up, only to break again
So much to check that I don't deviate from my lane
The room in which I'm stayin'
Adventure

The sun casts its reticent light
On the Campanile tower
But the light is a glimpse in time,
An impressionistic masterpiece, painted with watercolors
Fleeting and evanescent

And with this allow me to close
An unfinished tome
Of my life
For if I gain through every trial and tribulation
I emerge all the richer
And pure and beaming fields of daisies only I can picture
Through experience and innocence
I tread onward
Whatever the path

To that I say a resounding "I don't care"
I am here to carve a path of my own
It may not be as glamorous as yours, it may be rocky as
        navigating Piedmont in the evening
But it still remains a possession of mine
And that is a powerful possession.
And so through thick and thin
Though I go through days and weeks with hardly a grin
I continue to learn, and I continue to earn
Useful lessons that, if repeated enough times, will be
        mastered
Even with my enfeebled, recalcitrant mind
This is all mine

I owe it to myself and to those to whom I made a bitter vow
To pursue what I do, even if not to awe

I went through narrow heaven and ceaseless hell
I went through emaciation and hunger worse than words
    can tell
I went through bitter fights and tearful joys at rebuilding
    friendships
I went through bitter disappointments that pinned
    granite on my shoulders
And I went through the occasional rapture that led me to
    throw off the boulder
I went through failure, and will continue to do so
But I also know that I amass knowledge, and one fine day,
Not in the Gatsbyan veneer, but in mine . . .
It will be for the best
For God put me here on Earth to tackle what I've gone
    through
And the best I can do for myself and others
Is to continue to do.

The sun casts its reticent light
On the Campanile tower
But the light is a glimpse in time,
An impressionistic masterpiece, painted with watercolors
Fleeting and evanescent

To me it is the portrait of hope
But hope is fleeting
Can disappear with every academic meeting
Every whatchamacall unforsaken drama meeting
And yet it comes to symbolize the unlived dream
Impossible as it may seem

Wake up
Fields of daisies in my mind

Drawn out the bleak landscape dominated by a
　　grotesque math building
Everybody has a story
Time to wallow in everyone's glory
Maybe it will transfer to my own

The sun casts its reticent light
On the Campanile tower
But the light is a glimpse in time,
An impressionistic masterpiece, painted with watercolors
Fleeting and evanescent

To me it is the portrait of hope
But hope is fleeting
Can disappear with every academic meeting
Every whatchamacall unforsaken drama meeting
And yet it comes to symbolize the unlived dream
Impossible as it may seem

Day 1, it's inconceivable
The day was disingenuously ensconced until it
　　materializes with full fertility
My head bubbling skyward, toward the hazy clouds
As I find myself a speck,
A speck among 30,000 others
Simply walking alone, finding my daily routine
Among buildings that lay claim to their territory long
　　before I came here
And will be here long after I'm gone
So full of hubbub, yet quite alone
This is my time to shine
But as the bat fails to connect the ball
And miscalculates the upswing
So I, too, discount the upswing of arduousness

I have forgotten what it means to strive
It is in my past, in a foreclosed hive
What does it mean, I tell you, to spend ages
Taking a look, buried in every book
Searching for the answer
Fruitlessly
Awkwardly
And, finally, sputter
Light goes out
With utter intensity of my discombobulated spirit I
      bring forth the concrete demarcation of a scream
Voiceless scream
After all, what of my dreams
Didn't I come here to find myself
To grow, into uncharted territories to delve
Someone forgot to tell the engineering department not to
      admit me
And now I find me
Under lock and key
Struggling
Out goes this club, down with that one
But I can't let go so easily
It's entrenched in me, I'm imbued with it
I don't understand the idea of no extracurricular
      participation
In my mind it bears equivalency
With useless rumination, passivity never bore a high
      station
So I find myself in a slow, floundering wallow
Slow to react
And so concludes the aforementioned act

The sun casts its reticent light
On the Campanile tower

But the light is a glimpse in time,
An impressionistic masterpiece, painted with watercolors
Fleeting and evanescent

To me it is the portrait of hope
But hope is fleeting
Can disappear with every academic meeting
Every whatchamacall forsaken drama meeting
And yet it comes to symbolize the unlived dream
Impossible as it may seem

Step two.
Out of the shattered, ramshackle ruins of what could've
    been
If the recipe is correct, if one is right to act
In accordance and with respect
With proper steps and applications
On top of shards of salvaged physics midterm grades
Emerges a breath of new life
Beneath the dusky Nor Cal sky
Dreams are made running through urgent ideas
Urgent without cause, urgent without substance
A new girl, who is she?
The fiery, rambunctious anxiousness overwhelms
It consumes, but it's a desirable consumption,
Poetic conundrum, a sundry quandary to interpret
With every late-night rendezvous, the scarf of secrecy
    unveils a tad
But not enough for each party to lose interest
It regresses and returns, permanently sinusoidal
And hence every late-night rendezvous
Turns into rendezvous after rendezvous
Until the world is on its feet
Until the breath of life enters the skeleton of long-
    slumbering friendships

Again, now awakened
We are one!
We are one until the onset of the sun!
We are one against the bitter 24-7 workload, we will
    validate what it means to be fraternal
To join a fraternity and otherwise
Work my pass, but our camaraderie is eternal
But alas, crash, what now, whence did it stop
When did a grade so hard-earned begin to drop

One more time
With a deep, bitter, sonorous sigh
A replete regression into sorrow and misery
A poli sci major I want to be
So long as I fight with engineering classes, woe is me
I wasn't meant to be
Or just maybe I wasn't meant to shine
To be able to say mastery of the sciences, of glimmering
    universal secrets is thine
I give up, ok, I give up
What more do you want, haven't you had enough
My pain is your gain
You view me with disdain
I understand, and don't want to go to school
All I want is to sit on my stool
And stare into space
And think of what could've been and nevermore
And mice and men and where the story of their lore
May have differed, if . . .
But if is an abstraction, only offered as politically correct
    distraction.

The sun casts its reticent light
On the Campanile tower

But the light is a glimpse in time,
An impressionistic masterpiece, painted with watercolors
Fleeting and evanescent

To me it is the portrait of hope
But hope is fleeting
Can disappear with every academic meeting
Every whatchamacall forsaken drama meeting
And yet it comes to symbolize the unlived dream
Impossible as it may seem

Long-awaited break, then another
Then reentry to school
But those 4 weeks of freedom
Taught me a valuable lesson that all is not lost
From the ashes of mobilizing for the last 2 weeks of finals
Of somehow succeeding in pulling something off
I am endowed with the knowledge
That my days are numbered only if I want them to be
And that, my friend, is a powerful semantic convention
Which on cold, dark days serves to break the tension
For everyone is wonderful in their own way,
Naïve postulating, not enough to make it in this world?

Igor Tregub '07
POLITICAL SCIENCE

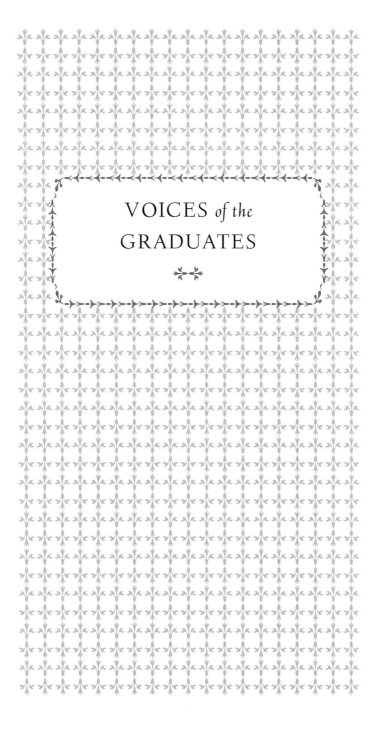

VOICES *of the*

GRADUATES

Tumble and Roll with Oski

Tumble and roll—tumble and roll
It's our Oski wanting the Rose Bowl
He is always on field at the game time
When we spot him all is fine

Tumble and roll—tumble and roll
This Oski is voiceless, like a troll
He shows curiosity, joy and no shame
In our hearts we feel the same

Tumble and roll—tumble and roll
Memorial Stadium is the shoal
Oski tumbles and lands upright
All the rooters feel pure delight

Tumble and roll—tumble and roll
Oski is ageless, eyes fixed on the goal
He is lovable, whimsical, sometimes blue
In his floppy shoes, Big C sweater of golden hue

Tumble and roll—tumble and roll
Oski is spirit, complete and whole
He is ready to cheer and laugh for joy
As he holds his round little tummy feeling coy

Tumble and roll—tumble and roll
Oski is cute and such a charmer droll
He inspires us to "GO BEARS" victory
He is a well-loved legend at UC

Jean Liu '39
PHYSICAL EDUCATION

The Final Frosh/Soph Brawl, 1937–1938

A littered lawn
'Tween Boalt and books
Brought smiling looks
At tattered shirts
Torn jeans and socks
Yes, even jocks!

Within the libe
Shoes shattered glasses
Spelling doom
For future classes.

Paul Williamson '40
ECONOMICS/BUSINESS
ADMINISTRATION

Cal 1943–1947

Memories of UCB:
Pledging a sorority,
Hiking up to the Big C,
Majoring in psychology,
Running down to LSB,
Research in the library,
Rooters' train to USC.
Attending many college dances,
Having several romances,
Sometimes taking risky chances.
Going to my Senior Ball,
Attending class in Wheeler Hall,
Football games in early fall.
Cheering in the rooters' stand,
Music of the great Cal Band;
It was always simply grand!
Many men were off to war
In the year of '44
But there were V-12s by the score.
Then a shout, a mighty roar;
Finally, at war no more!
Cal was peaceful, as before.
Study, school, time to play,
Working, too, to earn some pay.
Then graduation, the Big Day!

Reunion 2002

Hearing Campanile's chimes,
Recalling happy college times,
Visiting the campus still
Gives to me the same old thrill.

Phyllis Prindle Carvalho '47
PSYCHOLOGY

73

The First Ten Years
Are the Hardest

This is the story of one of our California Bears. This bear is a little girl bear, and we shall call her Mindie.  When she entered the University, she was happy and carefree. She did not yet know the hard life of a study (?) worn student. Until she became used to the campus hills, and the 10-mile hikes between classes, she found herself

and

in order to make classes on time. The main part of her college life consisted of

and

Then a *little*

and more

and

Of course, there were
the never-ending

with lengthy discussions about men, sex, and studies,
(in that order). For extra-curricular activities, there
were

and of course

Another part of
college life I am sure
she will never forget
are the beer busts

 and the morning after.

At the end of every
semester comes

a time of
horrible agony—
FINALS WEEK!!!!!!

But now she has
overcome it all
and is a

I am sure that when she is old and gray

she will never forget

and the good times
she has had there.

Virginia Mawdsley '47
PHYSICAL EDUCATION

Treble Clef

Love you, U.C. Berkeley.
The things we didn't do
For fun in Treble Clef.
So here are just a few:
Chants like "Walter, Walter,
Take me to the altar."
At football games we sang and flipped
Stunt cards—"never do we falter."
Riding rowdy rooter trains
To exciting Cal Bear games.
Pappy Waldorf led us on
To good ole U.C. fame.
Musicals at Wheeler Hall like
"The Judge Wore Black with Selected Shorts"
We always pleased our audiences.
Thank you for your support.

Mary Elaine Slater Jacobs '48
SOCIAL WELFARE

Kudos to a Bear Backer

To Gus Perscheid on his 77th birthday

Let's give a cheer for Gus, that loyal fan
Who, each fall, works on getting a tan
Sitting in that stadium called Memorial
Where the atmosphere usually is "funorial"
Because the home team invariably crumbles
When onto the field another team rumbles.
Biannually, Trojans come up from the south
Making Gus, the rooter, down in the mouth.
And the Bruins, although they're considered kin,
Always take great delight in doing the Bears in.
There are Beavers, Cougars, Wildcats, and Ducks
Who come to Berkeley just to have their yucks
From beating up the Bears in their own den,
As do the other members of the Pac-Ten.
Climbing the stadium steps, this alum so staunch
Forgets his creaky knees, ignores his paunch,
And looks forward to cheering on the blue and the gold,
Though he knows damned well they're destined to fold.
He's one of the faithful, one of the Cal die-hards,
Who calls Stanford the Indians instead of the Cards.
"Give 'em the axe," at the big game he'll yell.
"Chop down the Tree and burn it in hell."
But he knows all along that he's yelling in vain,
For when the game's over, there'll be that old pain
In his derriere from sitting and also in his heart
From backing a team that's still trying to start.
He'll go home that night and have himself a short beer,
This old Blue, this Cal guy, this not quite civil engineer.
Go Bears!

Art Poulin '48
PHYSICAL EDUCATION

To the Spirit of My Alma Mater

The embodiment of the spirit
Of U.C. Berkeley's fame
Is that of a fostering mother
My love I do proclaim
She bid me follow pathways
Of discernment and diligence
She led me through dark hallways with
Intelligence and patience
She beckoned me through new doorways
Of information and knowledge
The Pierian Spring overflowed
As she guided me through my college
She held my hand in times of stress
Her view was international
She introduced awareness
Of what was and was not rational
And though I never saw her
Her spirit was there, nearby
Understanding my fallowness
Encouraging me always to try
She nourished me when I faltered
She set me up after I fell
As love from a mother is constant
I soon fell under her spell
Through all the struggles and achievements
She taught lessons about integrity
For I was a young apprentice
Learning what it means to be free
Free to ask any questions
Free to express my view
Free to examine, reject, or support

Any thought, old or new
Free to explore new procedures
Free to uphold what is good
Free to allow other opinions
Which sometimes I never understood
Free to be a risk taker
Free to accept limitations
Free to enjoy all beauty in life
In all its manifestations
Now, in contemplation, I know
That commitment and conviction
Were stepping stones in the pathway
To her final benediction
Gladly I return to thank her,
To reinforce that which binds
And to revel in the company
Of fellow and kindred minds

Rocky Main '49
HUMANITIES

A Gingko Tree on
U.C. Berkeley Campus

there
is   a
glorious golden tree
still so alive for me
these many years
since first I glimpsed
its shimmering,
glittering glory
that I know
it will glow
and grow
ever so
long after all
the leaves fall
long after all
the
trees
fall
long
after
all

Bill Trampleasure '50
SOCIAL WELFARE

The Chosen Ones

In 1901 at Cal Berkeley
Women students were still rather rare,
But what they lacked in numbers
They made up for in wisdom and care.

They loved their dear Alma Mater
Just as we do today.
They wanted to serve her nobly,
Were determined to find a way.

They met with their favorite mentor,
Who strongly and wisely agreed,
There was work to be done by young women,
The campus had so many needs.

It needed an infirmary
And an adequate women's gym.
It needed more housing for students,
So "Let the great work begin!"

An honor society for women
Was founded and lives to this day.
Its motto is "Faith-Service-Loyalty"
Junior and Senior women hold sway.

For so many needs on campus
They raise the funds and more,
Health care, child care, housing,
Whatever comes to the fore.

* * *

So Cheers to Prytanean,
May it always thrive,
To keep the spirit of ancient Greece,
"The Chosen Ones" alive.

Elaine Hartgogian Anderson '52
ART/ART HISTORY

Ode to an Ol' Blue

It all began in the fifties,
Dad and our children were fans,
Family tickets admitted,
Two adults, three kids, in the stands.

Carol's girls each sat beside her,
Dad and I, my boys, would munch,
Sandwiches, cookies and peanuts,
Washed down with a soda, for lunch.

Soon the bomb awakened the Band!
Gold capes topped with feathered hats
Still serpentine the field of green,
Then pose, in an ocean of spats.

The anthem blared, the colors flew,
To the lyrics that enthrall,
Our kids could hardly wait to yell,
Go Cal! Go Oski! or, Play Ball!

Gridiron fortunes have spanned the years,
Dad died, kids grew—transition—
But through it all Carol and I
Upheld what was now tradition.

Forty years' worth of peanut shells,
Some hard-boiled eggs with salt,
We always took turns at half-time
To treat each other to a malt.

* * *

How we cheered when we were winning.
And how somber we could sit,
If at crucial times we'd fumble,
We'd say to each other, "Aw shit!"

This summer, Carol passed away,
Her cancer struck like a blow,
A lonesome "Ol' Blue" must root now,
And I'm going to miss her so.

The seat beside me lies vacant,
Carol's smile no longer there,
Yet far, from in the firmament,
I can hear her whisper, "Go Bear!"

Roland R. Bianchi '52
BUSINESS/PRE-LAW

Dirge on the Death of Harmon Gym

Alas, ole Harmon, we knew you well,
Your leather-lunged Vulcan's bellows silenced,
Dali-dead, straw hats muffled.

From ashes Mammon rises,
God of greed, Godot's supplications for naught,
As money lenders wrest the temple.

Alas, ole Harmon, we knew you well,
But not as well as Haas declaims,
Or pro scouts acclaim

Farewell, ole Harmon
Sixth man, invisible, but there,
Terrorizing opponents like an extra star.

Faint memory of your power,
So soon forgotten, your tradition gone,
Now pale phantasma of yore.

Farewell, ole Harmon,
We knew you well.

Jim Jenner '55
POLITICAL SCIENCE

He Never Registered

Near Sather Gate a fountain played
Around it students were arrayed.

The waters in the fountain danced.
We students watched and were entranced.

He was never late; he didn't go to school.
Yet he was smart and no one's fool.

All got to love him, small and big.
They called the fountain, his—LUDWIG.

*(In memory of the dog Ludwig, who was
"in attendance" in the mid-'50s to '60s.
He brought a lot of joy to us students.)*

Joseph Peter Simini '57
BUSINESS

Sather Tower

Forgotten title,
Tells
Nothing of
Obelisque grace,
Measured three hundred seven,
Freestanding tall,
Over all
Who come
Each fall.

They still keep coming
And
Gaze anew;
Notes of carillon peal
Beguile with
Melodic call
Over all
They join
Each fall.

The roster's grown from
Those
Who were there
When World War One began,
Trampling peace.
Youth heard the call
Over all;
Some joined
That fall.

And so, and so, now
Down

Through the years
Other wars followed,
Some at home,
In hallowed hall.
Over all
The ring:
Don't fall!

But we know it can't
It
Won't, not so
Silent, sentry duty
Leave to those who
In granite hall,
Over all,
Are flawed,
Who fall.

Though we remember
This
Straight arrow
In Italianate style,
With four faces, has
Known tragedy's pall,
Over all;
It's stayed,
Won't fall.

A brilliant white shaft,
Viewed
From the hills
Of San Francisco,
Like pure gold, though

Tested by fire, tall
Over all
And proud,
Can't fall.

Our Campanile!

Evelyn (Dessery) Sichi '59
ANTHROPOLOGY

Thoughts on the beginning
of fall semester, 1961

Dawns the morn with promise grisly
Grey the sky with moisture drizzly
Awaken students far too early
At this hour we feel quite surly
Campanile plays its tune
Calls us back—much too soon.

Donna Matlock Thompson '63
PSYCHOLOGY

Words penned on a spring evening while feeling somewhat depressed just before finals . . . 5–24–62

Hark! for shame!
Halt, there, semester!
I've caught you sneaking out on me unawares
While here I sit, and baby-sit.

"Snirk, snirk," he said to me.
"Sir," I said, "you must not speak to me that way."
But, "Snirk, snirk," he repeated
Glittering ghoulishly in the gloaming.
"Really, Sir," said I, stepping backward too quickly
And twisting my ankle in a hole left lying around
By some careless rabbit and forgetting my next line
     in the process.
"Snirk, snirk," he said again, menacingly
Munching on a Munchy-crunchy man.
Then I gave in to my destiny as I knew I must.
"Snirk, snirk," said I, while he twirled
Around like a top three times and became a turnip.
Then I went home and finished my last term
Paper of my senior year, whispering
"Snirk, snirk" all the while.
Unfortunately, I couldn't graduate, but it is
Very comfortable here, as the walls are
Padded in my favorite color: blue.

Donna Matlock Thompson '63
PSYCHOLOGY

Evensong

The Campanile carillon rings out
vespers amid stillness of after hours
embracing campus, a farewell between friends.

Near the Mining Circle swooping swallows
the same mesmerizing motion at sunset
as an evening long ago in Siena

with Tuscan choirs singing into night
immersed in summer—
the feast of St. John.

Now in twilight star jasmine bloom
five petals round a yellow star
all twirled in a bed of green.

I inhale fragrance and dance
round and round I twirl
until the final gong resounds.

Mary McCarthy '64
UNDERGRADUATE WORK

Late Bloomer

Sturdy and tall a late chrysanthemum
Stands defiant of the frost,
A lonely summer sentinel
In my winter garden.
Though storms have come with frost and snow,
A glow of purple bloom stands out
Against a sullen sky.
Then dark clouds lighten
And comes the sun.
Fiat lux!

Lorene A. Stranahan '64
BACTERIOLOGY

A Cal Acrostic

Unlike any other school in the nation
Cal offers the most unique education

Blue and gold evoke lasting admiration
Enduring memories of demonstration
Reading and writing and long computation
Kept us studying with deep concentration
Engaged in life-altering conversation
Learning with unbridled determination
Each new lesson gave us an affirmation
Yes, we owe Cal our fond appreciation

Sue Welsch '64
STATISTICS

Fall on Sproul Plaza
The leaves clattering across
A new semester

Doug Adcock '65
BUSINESS ADMINISTRATION

Overnight hard rain
Brings a perfect yellow ring
Of fresh ginkgo leaves

Doug Adcock '65
BUSINESS ADMINISTRATION

The Musician at the Berkeley Café

He plucks his golden mandolin
At a table to the rear
A bit of music as we wander in
But what's he doing here?

This place is just an old café
With a tiny outdoor space
And this is only just a normal day
So then we watch his face.

Not once does his mouth crack a smile,
Not once do his eyes look up.
We ask how could his time here be worthwhile?
Is there money in his cup?

So what strange story brings him here?
What sad tragedy of fate?
He is a man too young for life to fear
Or working time to hate.

Perhaps he moonlights here and then
He goes back across the street
To teach the college students once again
And silly deadlines meet.

Perhaps divorce has bitter'd him
He no longer has a place
The future seems now only cold and grim
He has to mask his face.

Perhaps some dread disease has left
Certain marks upon his health

So deep that as he plays he feels bereft
Of happiness and health.

We eat our meal and still he plays
We get up and pay our bill.
His downcast eyes don't reach to meet our gaze
We're sure they never will.

Gessica Johnston '65
VIROLOGY

Berkeley

City on a hill
your lights and Campanile bell
I remember
People fall
like petals on the street
their souls exposed
outside their clothing
ringed ears
burlap bodies
woven with threads
of many colors
I squeeze in my hand
the dust
of my yesterdays
I see me
tripping the sidewalk
innocence loving
broken and brown
like a daisy
Best not to come
back
to the twilight land
of emerging self.

Pamela Altfeld Malone '65
HEBREW

View from Ida Sproul Hall

The fog rolls out; the tide rolls in;
The foghorns cease their noisy din.
Mount Tam rises with majestic ease
To catch the sweet Pacific breeze.
San Francisco stands white and clean
Above the Bay so blue and green.
The Campanile chimes nine o'clock
While seagulls hover over the Rock.
The sun shines brightly on the Coastal Ridges
And glints off the towers of the long Bay bridges.
The Berkeley Hills stand stark and bold,
The backdrop for the Blue and Gold.

Diana Carolyn Ice '68
GEOGRAPHY

Printemps à Berkeley

The lacen monkey trees
Spread at springtime
and Berkeley sings for a time
To San Francisco

a romance born for my friend in the city
Forever dances in her exciting blue eyes of pearls

She turns her corners along her mountain ways,
and she knows
Looking through my rainbow.

Robert Denis Don '70
SOCIOLOGY

Lifers

Turn the radio off, ignition off,
exhaust off, exhale the doubt that whines,
Why here, why the hell not France?
Inhale Sierra Zen that presses,
Yes here, yes now, seven days
here-in-the-moment, now, hello.

Swallows to Capistrano, salmon upstream,
magnets to a summer mother lode,
patterned, annual, we come.
Away from bylines, deadlines, skylines,
off online, picket line, ticket booth,
up from gas pump, speed bump, boom box,
unpagered, unlasered, uncalculatored,
we come here, to this mountain.

Stripped to sunscreen and trail boots,
equipped with ball gloves and band-aids,
we commit our unplugged selves
to life performed live—no filters,
dimmers, no remote controls.
Why are we here? Because we're here . . .

because a morning chorus wakes us—
black-throated warblers, ruby-crowned kinglets,
and empty-bellied children chirping
to the beat of early tennis balls
and urgent feet on the bathroom path.

because in mirrors above communal sinks
abandoned last-year faces wait to take up
dialogs draped summer to summer amid
damp towels, make-up, razors, soap.

* * *

because a bell is rung and Cal alums
fit elbow to armpit on skinny benches
for eggs à la Pavlov or chicken déjà vu.

because on Sunday we think aloud
and sing in leaf-baffled phrases.
We bind ourselves with common chords,
unfurrowed faces, loosen limbs, flow words,
and, sun-dappled, creek-babbled, float.

because in sandy pits men of iron,
heavy-waist division, celebrate the
weightless roll of a skyward horseless shoe.

because rumpled angels tumble through us,
clean the bathrooms (more or less),
ring bells, run tournaments, dance and sing.
The uncombed, un-slept Generation Next,
afflicted with joy, addicted to chaos and dirt,
inflict upon us laughter and tears as if
they were our own children. And they are.
Or are they ourselves before they were our kids?

because a line of hikers chuffs uphill
like an untuned engine, with boots and hats,
puffing dust and conversation:
I think . . . I can . . . I am . . . I must. . . .
At the top, breathless, earthless,
they gasp or whisper a Kodak prayer:
Please, I must remember this.

because the diamond forever calls out
and softball diehards, maybe tie-dyed
but never tongue-tied, touch base
with tendons last tried last July.

Sunstruck, feverpitched, dirtstreaked,
hamstrung—hey batter-batter,
can it get any better than this?

because beneath an avalanche of stars
our ever-ready flashlights fasten us
to paths, prevent our being swept away,
stunned into star-studded oblivion.

because as days revolve we learn (again)
that life can be reversible, downright rehearsable,
if only for a week. A moment here
is last year, next year, hello-goodbye-hello.
We pack our pungent clothes, our bites and sprains
and head for three hundred and fifty-eight
days somewhere-else-in-the-moment,
for House and Garden, latte, New York Times,
Posture-Pedic, a peculiar lack of dirt.
Unwound, rewound, down the mountain we go.
Italy next July? I don't think so.

Judy Maher '72-'73
ENGLISH

Nurre Lost His Star

It was a day to remember when
My fostering mother had
CS powder dumped on her hospital from
A guard chopper.

Nurre lost his star over
That neurological gambit while
Patients in five pointed lungs
Gasped for games.

My knees suffered,
Nose trembled,
Hair stood at attention and
My skin was crafted by
A Chemical Corps chaplain.

The CS lingered in the stairwells of
Lucite, de Haviland and
Strawberry Cross for an
Itchin' number of days.

I stood on Tolman's shoulders
Searching for Sigmund but
Saw a semi-circle of third degrees
Armed with clavicles
Guarding Bowker's chapel.

Demonstrating student PROTESTANTS
Prepared with posters on steeples
Chanting anatomy

Marched across the battlefield
To pray at the digs of
Fostering mother's caretaker.

Flower girls stuck stems of
Blooms in the devotions of
Semiautomatics and almost
Got toothpicks in their adolescent
Rocker arms for meditations.

The serene brought
Sharp sticks to my eyes as
Rabid rebels sat on the grass and
Sang "America the Beautiful" to
The accompaniment of gas.

As I floated across the mustard field
I spotted a van of the guard and said,
"What the hell are you doing here, Sergeant?"
He was ready for combat
Dressed in his yellow clown gown.
"I came here to kill hippies like you, sir."

I must have blanched.
I clanked down the fright and
Hit the blacktop as
I watched political activists
Cornered then applauded with
Leaded walkie-talkies.

Rumors spread that the
Coca Cola Company was
Paying athletes to riot and

I volunteered to teach
Squads of investors
The Mickey Mouse Club song.

Blue meanies
Isolated berserkeley hammer heads and
Protective custody was
Scored on traitors to Cannabis sativa.

The toke that broke my
Hapless humpback's aims was
Gutted libraries, blackened stacks,
Buildings soaked in gasoline,
Shelved in glass and burned.

Tempus fugit (time flies).
O felix culpa (O happy fault).
My fostering ma's a phoenix.

Gerald Olson '74
EDUCATION/COUNSELING PSYCHOLOGY

A Tribute to Cal

Looking back, my days at Cal were joyful all those
 years
The friendships made, the football games that sometimes
 brought on tears
The choir, the band, the late-night crams that were a
 part of it all
Helped shape me into what I do today, in all things,
 great or small

My memories of Cal live on with visions of the
 Campanile,
Morning classes that stretched my mind and made me
 think more freely
The grand old buildings that still stand and those that
 are quite new
Though deep in my mind of yesteryears still are clear in
 my view

The university on the hill, my room with views of my
 favorite Bay,
Return to my mind quite often and I daydream a little
 time away
I return to the place where I dreamed of a future
 unknown
As I walked among the redwoods and secret places I
 called my own

I hope and dream that someday my children will feel the
 same
That they will enjoy the thrill of victory each time we
 win the Big Game

That when they walk across the campus, both pride
    and hope are there
And that they sense all the fullness of UC treasures
    that they might share

Hail to California! I give thanks for all those days
My heart sings a joyful chorus in, oh, so many ways
I rally round the banner when someone spins a UC tale
For with strength, love, and courage, we Bears will
    never fail

Andy Main '78
COMPUTER SCIENCE

Preface

What is it again?
How have you been?
Me? I kept on going
Now I'm in law school
Trying to learn the legal rule
But I'll always write
When I find the time
And can make a rhyme.
I was scared it's true
And every Monday was blue
But I did my best
And recorded it for you
Because regardless of the school
We all keep going
And "they" keep on throwing
This stuff at us
It's the same driver
Just a different bus
But I needed more help
Than when I was at 'Cruz
And was more selective
In methods I used
But that's true for us all . . .
Well, maybe not all?
At least those who hear a call
If you'll read on
And someone leads on
Maybe I'll make it
Maybe we'll take it
And nobody will have to fake it!!

Honorable Kelvin Filer '80

LAW

Thanx, Daddy

First time I failed
I was so down
I wanted to quit
And get away from it all.
But my daddy said
It's no big thing.
It happens to us all.
Andy, I just tripped
And didn't really fall.
'Cause I'll take it over
To replace the first time,
Can't let it mess with my mind.
I only needed one more point.
The test freaked me out, as "they" say.
I wanted to shout.
Even though I did my best,
I should have taken a rest.
But you learn the hard way,
That's what my daddy would say.
I know I did,
'Cause I'll relax this time
And just concentrate on mine.
But my daddy said it happens,
I was just caught by surprise,
The first of many tries.
Well, I've got to run
And prepare for the next one.
No lie, it's not fun,
But luckily I'm the son

Of a father who's number one.
I only hope I can be
Half of the man I see.

Honorable Kelvin Filer '80

LAW

The Year's Over

Got through the first year
Of this difficult task.
What you might ask?
Everybody knows it was hard,
And I expected it.
I was in the pressure pit
And many times got hit
By new material
That I was unfamiliar with.
But I studied hard
And tried to speak in class
The first time I was asked,
"Mr. Filer, what are the facts?"
I did okay,
At least that's what my friends say.
Yet the hardest parts
Were the exams we took
Which covered all the books.
I just hope I passed,
Whether it was first or last.
The grades aren't out yet,
But I wouldn't bet
Because you can't be sure
Of what grade you'll get.
But if I make it
I'm going to take it . . . back home.
If I don't?
Well, I won't.
But I'll try again
Because it isn't the end.

Honorable Kelvin Filer '80

LAW

Aubade

March 7, 1981

The trail up in the foothills
Snakes among eucalyptus,
Each weary trunk begrudging
The weight it has borne for years;
Surreptitious fog muffles
The flowing quick-silver beads
Dripping from the verdigris
Daggers which adorn the trees
Pretending to be just leaves.
No wind even hushes through
The close quiet of this dawn;
At the bend ahead a deer,
A magnificent elder,
Oversees his grazing clan.
I stop to stare not quite sure
Whether to retreat or not.
The deer, suddenly aware
Of my aimless intrusion,
Leap to refuge in the brush,
Consciously graceful in flight.

Jamie Rawson '82
HISTORY

Berkeley, January 1983

In the morning,
when the fog has crept up from the bay,
the Campanile stands
like a sand castle, half submerged
by the rising tide.

Neal Doying '84
ORIENTAL LANGUAGES/JAPANESE

Fiat Lux

I have never played football at Memorial Stadium
or at any stadium anywhere
to be perfectly honest.

Now, I know the pleasure of a muddy field
in Long Beach on a brisk Thanksgiving morning.
No crowds. Cold pizza. Wet beer.

But today I am driving with my wife
and son in our tan mini-van
up the 5 at 7

in the morning, the nectarine sun
so artful that even Los Banos glows
like a lit birthday cake

and my son is angry with his universe
of a blue Hot Wheels car
and lukewarm orange juice

and that his dad and mom are singing
"Fight for California," dad mumbling
the words; mom, a little off-key.

He's not hungry. He wants
"Hike," he says, "hike!"
And I give myself a wedge

of two seconds at Memorial,
Cal v. Miami, 1990, the sky as blue
as the Bay and Russell White

* * *

rolling over the Hurricanes
like a pinball. Like mercury.
Except in my eye it's me

Wearing number 4.
And I blink and it's my son
and he's hit me in the head

with his mini-football.
I say out loud, "Maybe you'll
play for Cal someday"

and how many other fathers
have said this and thought of
the steps to Moses Hall,

an autumn evening and the quiet
study of wind and all things Berkeley,
how my wife taught me between

the pine needles, the dim
of a small half moon,
the click-clack of a bicycle chain

and the waft of Blondies pizza what
a kiss is, and how I whispered
after my first breath:

"I'm hungry now."

Michael Melo '91
ELECTRICAL ENGINEERING

I make my way up Bancroft,
up past vendors selling
bagels, kimchee, fried rice,
the hot oil smell like sweat
in the motionless air,
past the flower man,
gold teeth glinting when he smiles.

The clouds are low and flat,
the air beneath them nearly palpable
with heat and moisture,
luring me to sleep away the rest
of the afternoon.

On the grass below Hearst I sit,
sphinx-like,
watching the traffic below me
and the progress of the inchworm,
applegreen,
struggling over my bare toes.

On the grass it's cooler;
an almostbreeze fingers my hair,
caresses my half-closed eyelids.
A bee buzzes around my ankles,
seeing things my way.

Jeni Paltiel '94
ENGLISH

Voices

Sat facing the tides
on the steps 'side thee.
With the sun fallen o'r the gate
and my heart friends besides,

a shooting star flew by
and whispered just to me.
Felt I luck of mammoth fate,
uttered not a cry.

Being the needle in the stack—
just that single tower.
Knowing that you're found
when you hear that single crack:

of when laughter starts to peal,
shaking pollen off a flower.
Beholding a glorious sound
I sit under thee—campanile.

Oh, star of glorious prose
saying what I did yet know:
No other place be I rather
than with the love of those

Voices in the air,
my friends in tow.
Sitting under Sather
with each of you—there.

Daniel Orjuela '96
MATH/DRAMATIC ARTS

berkeley inamorata

What will i think of
when i think back on these fugitive years
among this land? will i remember
the roots of oaks
flexing through the sidewalks
where i walked
looking into windows
of wood shingle and brick houses,
cats on leaf-covered curbs, blooming
rosemary spilling over everywhere.
how could i forget the
yellow gingko leaves, the yellow
gingko leaves. or the persimmon tree,
in front of the light green house,
the spine of branches arching, heavy.
the rain, random commas, pausing
at the bend of the bursting heart fruit
before falling in front of me,
to the right. some things stay
with a person: the red breasted robin
perched in a leafless tree, the hands
of a man i loved, patient and itinerant,
poppies growing wild at the side of the road.

Theresa Tran '97
ENGLISH LITERATURE/CREATIVE WRITING

Graduation

The shawerma is far past grease now, its fat having
    slowly
Fallen from its layers, so it stands lean and unlovely,
Roasted tenderly, turning and turning in the window
    on Durant.

Slowly carving these slices away, the man stands humming,
Knife falling along the sides of the pillar, trimming,
    shaping,
Like a potter turning a slender pot between her knees.

In a cloud of heat and spice, I head across campus,
    chewing slowly.
Four years have fallen like the quiet leaves from the elms.
Even now, the earth is turning gradually toward the sun.

The pond's slow shimmer is gone from the Mining Circle.
Each minute is sliced clean and falling from the hour
By the turning of the Campanile's sharp and clever hands.

Slowly, the luxury has melted from the meat. Does the
    flesh
Remember the days before its fall, the marbling of fat,
    of youth,
The first moment its raw surface turned to meet the flame?

It roasts slowly on its silver axis, tree-ring pieces
Falling from the core. Through the night, as I walk home,
It is still turning, like the moon, like the lean and aging
    planets.

Huan-Hua Chye '01
LINGUISTICS

Yelp

For the Chancellor

I bear witness to the degeneration of the mind lying,
    both individually and
    collectively, in the student body,
dressing their limp, vegan, protein-deficient bodies in
    bright, vibrant colors of pinks,
    reds, oranges, and greens,
who dress "internationally" or culturally aware—
    American moms wearing elaborately
    designed saris, queer engineering majors strutting
    kimono garb, Muslim women—an ocean of long,
    flowing scarves
    and even longer more flowing cloth gowns,
or oftentimes to be the most radical, wear nothing at all
    and claim it to be a political right, even an
    obligation,
who gather on Telegraph and Bancroft and Durant
    waiting for spare change for dope,
who howl and scream and yelp in the dregs of the cool
    San Franciscan air,
who drink and drink and drink on Dwight till all they
    can see is the fluorescent glimmer
    of the Cody's bookstore sign,
who sell bumper stickers stating defiantly "Question
    authority!" and "Peace on Earth,"
who read your palm for free as the light changes,
who will do mehndi or body-piercing or get you a joint
    while you wait for a Veggie
    Special at Blondie's,
who play the harp and the sitar and Peruvian chants and
    reckless bucket-style drums to

an innate groove that makes your hips shake and
your toes tap,
who zealously hand out fliers on Sproul Plaza urging you
to become a Hindu, a Jew,
a Korean Protestant Christian, a transvestite,
a socialist, a democrat, a human,
who look at you from the steps of the ASUC and the
white pillars of Upper Sproul,
who hate conformity,
who despise Bush,
who scorn America,
who breathe, act, live, and die for some cause or another,
who go to class and lecture and lab and discussion day
after day without
thinking or reflecting or even learning,
who drink coffee at Café Strada and study at Doe and
watch movies at Wheeler,
who lie and lie to your already desensitized cerebral
cortex,
who like to smoke weed and smoke weed and then,
you guessed it, smoke weed, till
life is one long, perpetual high,
who want to sleep with one another like goddamn
rabbits
then sell their precious ova to help couples who
only wish for the joys of
holding their own, very own, child and call it
"my baby"
and mean it with true virtual reality love or the
pseudo–New Age version of it,
who argue with Rick Starr and Preacher Eddy and
Yoshua and the Hate Man and the
homeless bums and even, you, Chancellor,

who came to Cal with visions of pro-choice, affirmative
    actionary, hyper-politically
    active society,
who know no other inclination than the surreal
    ultra-left, ultra-right version of political
    science of our beloved alma-mater, Cal,
    in the God-Bless-United States of
    America,
yet are duped like children in urban angst.

How can you take my pain and strife and suffering
    and convert it to political self-
    righteousness?
How dare you take the history of my people and rewrite
    it, conveniently leaving out the
    lynchings, the torture, the injustice, the genocide?

But I'm desperately trying to make a difference
when I'm a dollar short and a day late and a block away
yet I trudge on, like a boat against the current,
or perhaps more accurately like an absurd animal in a
        strange universe
until death creeps on me like a shadow
and overtakes me like a wave
till the shock overwhelms me completely
and I am left to myself and to the darkness of the
    unknown and the
    uncertainty of the destiny of my After Life and
    to the judgment of God

Ah, Chancellor—you can and will and must worry
    about your free-thinking, liberal
    students.

Though they care, oh mighty chancellor, about ozone
    and bioengineering and
    euthanasia and poverty and hunger,
their will is not enough.
It never was.
It never could be.
I wish it was.

Sameena Azhar '02
PHILOSOPHY/PUBLIC HEALTH

Class Reunion

What greater reward in this land of the free
Than to be an alumnus of dear old UC.
Others may boast and laud in detail
Of days spent on campus at Harvard or Yale,
But the wondrous dreams of our fine future fate
Began on the day we first crossed Sather Gate.
To be sure, there were moments that did slightly pall
After hours of lectures in old Wheeler Hall,
But they soon passed away in our chatty lunch times
In the new Stephens Union where we heard the chimes
Of bellringer Murdock, campanile's grand master,
Playing "All Hail to Cal," or some songs students asked for.
Weekend recreation we often did seek
Strolling Faculty Glade on up to the creek
Known as Strawberry then, nor were buildings on hand—
You just skinny-dipped and admired the land.
On each Friday night, with your favorite date,
Five bucks and fruit punch meant Mark Hopkins 'til late.
If "Dancin' with Anson" made you forget the hour
So you missed the last ferry, then you prayed for the power
To get your gal home without driving too fast
Before that old needle said "You're out of gas."
We'd survived the Depression and had no laments;
Our hourly wage was twenty-five cents.
So in twenty long hours, if you labored hard,
You could earn enough bread for a student body card.
The Life Sciences Building appeared our first year—
Future doctors and nurses for its labs gave a cheer,
And others whose work would be dealing with science
Were jubilant as they used each new contrivance.
The MBA seekers frequented South Hall,

That venerable, most ancient building of all.
Those longing for licenses as engineers
Haunted Hesse and Hearst halls all four of their years.
A shingled North Hall provided the decks
For those who expected to be architects.
Those called to teaching used Haviland Hall
To learn how to keep school kids under control.
The present Boalt Hall would lay in the shade
The place used by those who would give legal aid.
The boys in the Band had no fillies on hand,
The Glee Club, likewise, thought "men only" was grand.
But women musicians, despite this, prevailed;
In Treble Clef concerts they often regaled.
Greeting students in weather both clement and foul
Were the fine, friendly features of Robert G. Sproul.
Our achievements scholastic and creations esthetic
Were outshone by far by our prowess athletic.
Our football team in '31 stopped Stanford in its tracks
After eight straight years of losses, they brought home
      the Axe.
'Twas retained by a tie in the year '32,
When all the world's presses were praising our Crew.
The Classes before us were 61, and 67 followed,
But we know the truth at our campus, now hallowed.
If all those Classes were put to the test
Our own '33 would prove to be best!

Wilma M. Avery Fay '33
BIOLOGY

68th Reunion Rejuvenation

Hail to California for we have all arrived
To celebrate our 68th reunion.
Grateful to God to be the members who've survived
And eager to start on our verbal communion.

As we face each other the visions we now see
Are so colored by our very warm affection
That faces lose their lines and all forms are fault free
Just models of utter delightful perfection.

More youthful odd strangers might notice urgent need
For facelifts, massages, long sessions in a spa,
Or miles on a treadmill, or reduction of our feed.
But we'll still sing "All Hail" and at games shall hoorah!

The wise human spirit transcends all gross matter,
Holds bright new ideas and expresses elation,
Whatever the body, though thinner or fatter,
We have all been reborn by our choice education.

So "Hail" boys and girls of the Class '33
Our attitudes super, our hearts very gianty.
We will eat, and we'll drink a grand toast to U.C.
Just like twenty-year-olds, though we're nudging ninety.

Wilma M. Avery Fay '33
BIOLOGY

69th Reunion Class of '33

We've come to shout our last hurrah
And though to these ancient deaf ears
It may seem faint and somewhat blah
Within our hearts it is husky as bears.

These limbs which once raced campus cross
Are now very worn and unstable,
Our lack of slender forms, a loss
But our brain cells are active and able.

We recall with joy those hours we spent
In Morrison Libe reading prose and verse
Knowing better now how much they meant,
Though then our jobs and classes came first.

At all big games we yelled 'til hoarse
Anxious to keep that precious axe,
Our curses on Stanford a matter of course,
In backing our teams we were never lax.

At last when we rose to get our degrees,
Secure the world's knowledge was held within,
We felt our future would prove a breeze.
We all know now, the struggle it's been!

Thanks be to God that we're still here
And our beloved Cal is thriving!
We're ready for that interview
With St. Peter soon to be arriving!

Wilma M. Avery Fay '33
BIOLOGY

Class of '33
Our 70th Reunion

We're here for our 70th and what could be neater
We managed to table that talk with St. Peter

To be sure there are walkers and canes near at hand
But for something this vital we each one shall stand

In nineteen hundred thirty-three when entering Sather
    Gate
Our voices dwelt on our exams and the thrill of our
    latest date

Today when we meet or sit down for a talk
We boast how our latest great-grandchild can walk

We used to sit in the stands and then jump up to loudly
    scream
Fighting words of encouragement to our winning
    football team

Today while ensconced in an ample divan
With glasses & hearing aides we've been forced to put on

We observe our eleven and relish the scene
As it's pictured for us on a wide T.V. screen.

But the last round-up's over, 'twas for us the bell tolled
Our hearts stayed in springtime but our bodies grew old.

Allegiance forever! Hail to Cal in ought three
Our ties will not sever while we have progeny!

Go Bears!

Wilma M. Avery Fay '33
BIOLOGY

At One Hundred . . . I Remember

One hundred years . . . I marvel at all about me.
Roses in bloom . . . gentle breeze stirs perfume.

A fluffy cloud settles around me . . .
A deep breath . . . I see a girl of seventeen
In awe of Sather Gate . . .
Entering her new world . . .
Its joys . . . sorrows . . . excitements . . . challenges.
My Alma Mater holding me close
For five fruitful years.

I remember the Parthenaea in Faculty Glade
Coeds in Grecian robes . . . dancing the ancient ballet.

A cloud blurs my vision.
SMOKE . . . FIRE . . . out of control
Blackening the eastern hills
Once carpeted with grass and golden poppies . . .
Raging down . . . voraciously devouring
Every structure . . . bush . . . tree in North Berkeley.

As if by magic . . . the fire burned itself out
At the border of the campus.

On the morrow . . . from the top of the Campanile
Through smoky clouds drifting by
I glimpsed a war-torn wasteland . . .
Scorched chimneys . . . tendrils of smoke
Charred black sticks . . . once beautiful trees.

Again I am lost in my little cloud.
When it disperses I clearly see a Junior . . .

Energetic, confident, happy
Receiving a scholarship . . .
Pinned by the Music Honor Society
Concerts . . . Theater . . . Football.

Through another wispy cloud I see Memorial Stadium.
Cal's Wonder Team of '24 . . . bonfire rallies
Coach Smith . . . Brick Mueller's longest pass ever.

The stadium fades away.
Greek Theater comes into view,
Center of academic, theatrical, musical events
On the stage, close to the piano
My violin and I solo . . .
Velvety tones reaching up to the sky . . .

My misty cloud dims the Greek Theater.
Suddenly . . . there I am . . . a Senior
Focusing on finals . . . farewells . . . the future . . .
SENIOR WEEK . . . Maytime . . . decisions
Farewell to Alma Mater . . . all places on campus
Women in white with white parasols . . .
Men in Cal blue jackets . . . white slacks . . .
The Senior Prom . . . magical night . . . Fairmont Hotel
I gowned in '20s modish knee-length dress . . .

GRADUATION . . . my dream fulfilled . . .
Donning caps with golden tassels . . . gowns . . .
Singing as we process in the stadium
"O God Our Help in Ages Past"
Diplomas in hand
Presented by Alma Mater's President.

My little cloud draws me to Sather Gate . . .
Looking back . . . framed in the Gate

The Stadium . . . the Greek Theater . . . the Campanile . . .
Gradually fade from view.

No clouds . . . a gentle breeze stirs the roses . . .
Wafts perfume . . . a cricket chirps . . . my garden . . .
Here I am at my desk . . . pen in hand . . .
Thank you . . . Alma Mater . . . for these precious memories

    Go Bears!

Reva Coon '25
ENGLISH/MUSIC

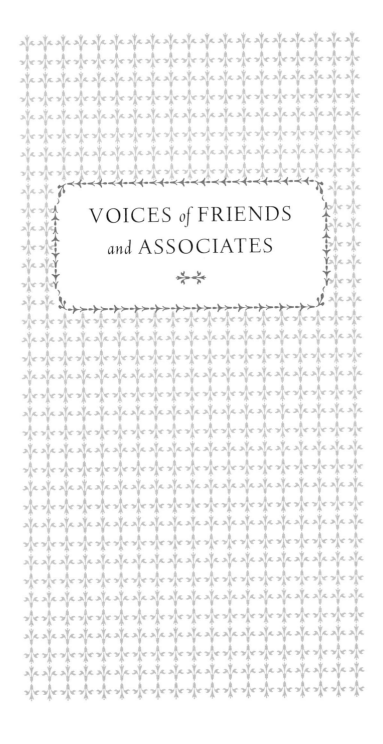

VOICES of FRIENDS
and ASSOCIATES

First Kisses

The Botanic Garden was moist
from record rains,
branches thick
with tiny purple flowers
we'd never seen before. Their aromas
trickled up into the air.

We sat on wooden steps
overlooking the whole canyon
with a view all the way to the Bay,
houses spilling up
the hills of San Francisco,
where we live apart.

When you kissed me
I thought of those Flemish Annunciations,
the angel both female and male
with long trills of hair—
your tongue fluttering
but determined.

Zack Rogow
UNIVERSITY ASSOCIATE

Blackout

Some little rat gnawed through a cord
and shut down the whole university.
All our work leveled
like an earthquake
that shakes everything evenly.

All our computers suddenly black.
Whirring fans silent. Lights out.
If this were the desert,
we'd be happy for stars.

And it is a desert.
The mummies live in the sands of academia.
Only a dead painter can paint.
Only a dead sculptor can bring clay to life.

We admire the dead,
as if they are somehow more alive than we
who carve their words in granite
and chisel their names on stone.

Art is rarely loved when it is conceived.
First it has to rot,
be forgotten,
then dug up again—white bones.

Padma Rubiales Rajaoui
UNIVERSITY ASSOCIATE

Nonconforming under plums

Prim and proper smartish
students of satori sat
dreaming of long afternoons
and red red valleys of home.

Smiling we watched them,
thought of Sartre,
his "Being and Nausea,"
or was it Frost
and "Mending Wall"?

How much they miss,
these meditators, avoiders
of sensation, stonefaced
in the longish moon,

missing in Berkeley
an obvious path-
seeing-in-being-in-bliss.
How? Why? It's July!

Larry Ruth
UNIVERSITY ASSOCIATE

Strawberry Creek

banks partly concretized, shored up
a scattering of rocks and pebbles for a bed
overhung by bay, maple and redwood
ivy clambering down dirt slopes like curious boys
sometimes clear and musical
sometimes cloudy, sluggish and quiet
a bird flutters down and inspects you
or a squirrel comes to visit you
a raucous jay calls then is silent
sunlight streams through a mazeway of branches
in a broken pattern
a low concrete fall barely a foot high
spills water from a sluggish pool
in a number of small, silvery falls
the water striders enjoy the sun
where are they?
ancient blocks of concrete disrupt your flow
here is a branch of eucalyptus broken off
and fallen in you, contributing its flavor
to the weak tea you carry to the sea
now here you go under one of many bridges
you were named for the strawberries that lined your banks
but i have yet to see a single strawberry
i follow you upstream, you are clearer here
less put upon
the strong roots of old trees stabilize your banks
better than concrete
the air is still here under them
still and quiet
the feisty winds have been trapped in loving branches
and stilled like a child trapped in her mother's arms

all around the noise of machinery
the temporary human noise of the city
your banks suddenly get steeper
I am looking down from a greater height
more redwood trees appear, they stand as guardians
guardians of your music, your flow
i am walking on a carpet of their leaves
the ground suddenly springy beneath my shoes
o look! you are suddenly in sunlight
you seem happy for it
i continue my slow meander
pausing every few steps to say something about you
someone has left a painting at the base of a redwood
just above you and there is a metal shed
i walk toward it out of the shadows into the sunlight
i see more concrete set into the earth
now into the shade again i glimpse a pipe
straddling your banks carrying something somewhere
more concrete interrupts your flow, a broken wall
meant no doubt to slow you down, to tame you
when you are at the fullest, rushing seaward
i walk thru the park-like redwoods
i see the buildings spring up on your farther bank
i note that your floor is partly concrete
and how this interrupts your flow and makes deep pools
over which the water striders skitter and dance
i see a plastic bottle hung up on a rock
i see the green of algae
an artificial stairway becomes your path
with every now and then a piece of junk
and the ever-present green of algae
here the grass grows down right into you
the crab grass tickles you with its fingers
now you duck under a bridge with a huge arch

so huge i saunter down and walk below
then back again
i am following you following you
here you are spread out here you are confined
then spread out again
another fall and another, each higher than the last
a dorito bag waits in you for the next big flood
you will wash it away when the winter rains appear
here you are grown so narrow i leap across you
and see two dragonflies chasing each other
when i climb the bank
you are becoming more mysterious, less open
i expect to see you disappear entirely
before too long
but first i come to a good place, where wild blackberries
festoon your farther bank with blossoms and fruit
pink green red and black
and now a plant whose name i do not know
fern-like growing in you, could it be watercress?
the smell of tea has grown stronger here
but you are more quiet
you are taking it easy, gathering your strength
i see you disappear around the bend
and follow, and see a thicket of horsetails
and more blackberries
another stone wall to interrupt your flow
your channel is carefully plotted
i climb your bank there is an area i can't pass thru
but you manage to
the smell of oak and bay are thick in the air
elderberry and holly become your neighbors
i see where one of your banks is shored up
with a wall of sandbags
i see you go much farther than i can follow

i see your path become darker, more treacherous
i feel i do not really know you
an unnamed plant with trumpet-like red blossoms
suddenly appears at the entrance of another arch
out of sunlight and in again out and in again
you have a biography like anyone yet who knows it?
i have perhaps written a small chapter of it
oak, and redwood, and bay

Dennis Fritzinger
UNIVERSITY ASSOCIATE

On Berkeley Campus

Tall and slender eucalyptus,
    Colored softly green or blue,
Peeling bark and scattered leaflets,
    Wind-tossed toys of somber hue.
Watching o'er the Berkeley Campus,
    Guarding ever night and day,
Visioning scenes of gorgeous beauty,
    Scenes of green and gold and gray.

Fog-dripped, misty eucalyptus,
    Roots firm planted in the earth,
Inspiration to all about you,
    In dreamy moods or moods of mirth.
Feathery tops are gently swaying,
    Odorous breezes through them play.
Gnarled or straight we love you truly,
    Let your forms be what they may.

Do you listen, eucalyptus,
    As Campus bells peal forth their lay,
Or are your thoughts far in the distance
    As you gaze out o'er the Bay
To the Gate of Gold, oh eucalyptus,
    Where ocean foam breaks into spray,
And a fog-bound sun drops gently downward
    To a bed of glistening-gray?

Tower you high, oh eucalyptus,
    Purpose, hope, and love inspire,
Plumy crests of creamy blossoms
    Raise our thoughts up ever higher.

Beauty round you, eucalyptus,
　　As you stand with kingly air,
Guarding well the Berkeley Campus,
　　With its treasures, fine and rare.

Clara L. Lowry
FRIEND OF THE UNIVERSITY

Produced by Wilsted & Taylor Publishing Services,
Oakland, California
PROJECT MANAGEMENT: Christine Taylor
PRODUCTION ASSISTANCE: Andrew Patty
COPYEDITING: Melody Lacina
DESIGN AND COMPOSITION: Melissa Ehn
PRINTING AND BINDING: Thomson-Shore, Inc.